SUNDRY ABDUCTIONS

SUNDRY ABDUCTIONS

Maria Dylan Himmelman

Hanging Loose Press,
Brooklyn, New York

www.hangingloosepress.com
Printed in the United States of America 10 9 8 7 6 5 4 3 2 1

Hanging Loose Press thanks the Russell Freedman Foundation and the
Literature Program of the New York State Council on the Arts for
grants in support of the publication of this book.

Cover art: *Boy with Pigeons*, Richard Haines
Design: Nanako Inoue
Author photo: Yisroel Teitelbaum
Photo on page 1: Ralph Ditter (1966), Bettmann Archive via Getty Images.

ISBN 978-1-934909-75-1

For Alessandra

First Annual Founders Award

Hanging Loose is proud to publish *Sundry Abductions*, the first winner of our newly established Founders Award. Russell Freedman, the late distinguished author of history books for young adults, had been a friend of Hanging Loose since we started in 1966. We are grateful to the Russell Freedman Foundation, which generously established the Founders Award. This annual award for a first book of poems honors the memory of three Hanging Loose founders: Ron Schreiber, Emmett Jarrett, and Robert Hershon.

Contents

Hiraeth . . . 3

A CARELESS COSMIC MISTAKE

ON THIS LOST PLANET

TEN THINGS were created on the eve of the Sabbath at twilight, and these are they:

[1] The mouth of the earth, [2] the mouth of the well, [3] the mouth of the donkey, [4] the rainbow, [5] the manna, [6] the staff, [7] the shamir, [8] the letters, [9] The writing, [10] and the tablets. And some say: also the demons, the grave of Moses, And the ram of Abraham, our father. And some say: and also tongs, made with tongs.

—Pirkei Avot 5:6

Hiraeth

In pursuit of something I couldn't name
I wandered the home store, while two men

from São Paulo sang of a place they wouldn't find
and a woman from Cardiff, her hair tangled like

the moor and heath too distant to return to,
shattered her teacup, and a clerk shouted

that there was need for immediate cleanup in the Aisle
of Unpronounceable and Insatiable Longings

The Majesty of It All

The Real McCoy

Rum-running is the act of smuggling liquor over water
Bootlegging refers to smuggling liquor over land
Brazenness and optimism, while not official terms,
apply to the man who took a flask of the Führer's
finest Cognac straight from the Eagle's Nest
and years later poured it into a small silver cup
to toast the guests at his eldest son's Bar Mitzvah

After they bury me I suppose they will toast
my unparalleled capacity for wasting time or my
proclivity for spinning wild yarns, and of my soufflés
they will say what they must. I'm not one to traffic
in pedigree, but I'd like it mentioned that William McCoy,
no relation, was a devoted family man and never
watered the hooch. Uncork the best bottle! Pour
your finest brandy! Raise a glass to this life in which
strangely each day somebody dies

Dinner with the Oligarch

His mother is no longer crouched
in a tiny birch house, eating potatoes under
dim country light. She is in London now,
tableside with her son, the donkey, in a stable-
sized dining room, smoothing his silk suit
while he snorts and breathes through stained
crooked teeth. His wife the thoroughbred
wears a plate of jewels bridled across her delicate
chest. Her four well-groomed ponies stand by
her side while we the guests sit palm on palm,
silent at the shrine of his half-drunk glass
of apple brandy

The man who once slipped

into the yawn of a rocket
and flew through heaven in a suit of balloons
now sits stooped and alone at the party
while the rest of the guests sip and nibble
on crackers with cheese

They are content with their lot, but
he could not look more out of place
if he had fish for fingers
as he stares through a window
at the full sturgeon moon

Juana Maria

The last of her kind
alone and naked on a slice of *terra firma*
in the roiling Pacific. Her broken footmarks
in sand as revealing as print on the page
to the sailors stinking of whale sperm
and ambergris who covered her with trousers,
a soiled blouse, and sailed her to civilization

We rescue the shoeless and Godless
those who suffer distocic births, yet:
(here the choir chimes in) who will save
those among us so impoverished
they have only money?

In the Village of Naysayers

At night the men leave their hats
facedown on the table, choosing not
to catch even a morsel of heaven's bounty

The teacher explains to her pupils
that endless sunshine creates a desert, while rain
falls on eaves sharp as knives

A soldier spared when the bullet
intended for his back strikes instead the fish
tinned in his rucksack, complains that

his lunch was ruined

Adrift

I spent an afternoon in Portugal with a dead man
I'd been watching surfers tempt fate
on the big waves in Nazaré when he approached
holding a bowl of offal. *I'm Tony*, he said
as he stuck out his hand. *Tripe? Tongue?*
He offered me a forkful and started to talk about
about all sorts of things—heroin, television
the street vendors in Queens. He said he'd been recently
undone by a cruel and unfaithful woman
and was flying off in the morning. He missed his daughter
From this high up you can only go down, he said
It was getting dark, the surfers were heading home,
boards tucked under their arms. A small collarless dog
strolled by, a piece of driftwood in his mouth

To What End

Imagine you are the first to conjure numbers
raising a finger and choosing one for yourself
two for your lover and as an afterthought,
three for the stranger glaring from across
the dying embers. You must then count things
like box cutters and telephones and know
that an elephant is composed of exactly
one million stars. Like sand, you will be
endlessly forced to solve complex equations
and to try explaining fractions to seashells

Revelation

It starts with a marionette, a veil, a man in a suit
There is often a woman, a fish, and you
can hardly tell one from the other

Angry clouds on a scrim,
the actors mime fear in a storm
the audience is drenched in the downpour

For the finale a hand in the wings
pulls on the curtain
and the whole blistered world is revealed

and ashamed of its nakedness
When it is over the players return
to their offstage lives

Stories like this

all begin the same way. The sow is snoring
under a quilt when the meteor
breaks through the roof and strikes
her limb. The wound is usually shaped like a cross
or a pineapple. The papers are called
and the curious drive by
The swaybacked mare from next door
claims the meteor belongs to her
The dying star is always left on the floor
to smolder like yesterday's headline
The boar leaves his wife for
a much younger pig

The Majesty of It All

Almost dark and she shouldn't care that he bends
like an old flower to polish his gun, takes off
like buckshot to hang
by his knees from the trees
He can stay out all night shooting
pool and spending
time with the ladies. Here at home
coffee stales in the pot, the old hen has laid
her last egg, and the TV says the Queen
has decreed that the price of love
is grief. After she sweeps
she'll take her worn hat from its hook
and wear it out back like a crown

Tithe

Luck is unexpected like breaking
an egg and finding two yolks

Fortune is brassy and proud
and tends to beget
Celebrity and bewildered offspring

Fame requires the famous to give their lives
to the audience
or at least ten percent of any
near drownings or sundry abductions

Burning Craters

Some of the things I have failed to attain:
a bell for each toe, pages filled

with glamorous truths, an antidote
for the curse of wandering

when expelled from the homeland
Like a methane crater set ablaze—

decades later there are holes in my life
that still smolder with want

I long for a house in the Biglands
or wherever it is

that the best burning craters are found

I want every windowsill filled
with wishbones

I wish to believe that
what I already have

is enough

Off the Record

This, Too, Is off the Record

Of course I wanted to see where the oceans meet
find me a good paparazzo who doesn't

This is news that breaks like a wave—a scandal
that churns: the wild tangle between the lusty

silt of the Indian and the cool longing
of the frigid Atlantic. Months on that boat—

miserable dinghy, barely seaworthy, to say nothing
of the boredom and spoiled wine that was

no balm for ambition. Imagine my disappointment
dropping anchor at the edge of the continent,

only to have a shrill, bent woman click her tongue
to tell me in Xhosa that oceans are shy, their exchanges

private, while behind me the water became frantic
and tried to blend in with the sky

It Could Be Worse

You could have fallen down the well
and had to be rescued
while the world watched on TV
or been mistaken for dead
and spent the night alone
on a slab in the morgue

Sometimes you miss your flight
and the plane crashes. Sometimes
the man on the street with a knife
is simply a chef

The police have caught the hoodlum
who defaced the trees in the park
with the word DONE,
motive unknown

Turn off the lights when you leave

Fighting Words

The battle was awful
but worse were the thumps and flops

of those clumsy apologies and awkward excuses
They kept me awake all night

so I grand-juried every last one
and threw them in jail

I regret to report that early this morning
they were paroled

by a dishonorable judge
and they are back on the street

looking to brawl

Always a Mercy

Tomorrow always packs a fresh challenge in her pocketbook
and prayer is rarely answered by the party you are calling
Listen to someone who has been around awhile
after all, it takes a hundred-year drought
to expose the remains of a shipwreck
Something else I want you to know—
sawfish have lips as luscious as a mango
and it's almost always a mercy to be
denied the things you want most
I remember after the war
women drew lines down the backs
of their legs, then went into the street
and kissed perfect strangers
God I hope that doesn't happen again
No shoes on the couch. Peels in the trash

The World's Loudest Sound

Where she came from, they waited for weeks
after the reactor exploded to bury
rows of rotting cabbages and nodding birch trees
then they commanded the soldiers
to bury the dirt

She told me to keep one good friend
As everyone will need someone to bury them

That old Greek monk whose mother died
giving birth to him was buried
by his entire order, who believed him to be
the only man in the world never
to have set eyes on a woman

The sound as they lowered his casket
cheer or lamentation
must have been as loud
as a house full of screaming children

The eruption of Krakatoa destroyed
many an eardrum, she'd say
You should never know from such a noise
She was Mother Superior
in a housecoat. Her brisket buried
in fried onions was more holy
than a psalm

Though They Suffered a Great Thirst

They broke stones with hammers
during the longest long winter, and under the trees
they unloaded piles of piles

When flakes landed on their striped prison cuffs
they lifted their heads
to catch snow with their mouths

There was a day and the deep pull of sleep
when she fell. A sprawl
of tatter and limb, when she fell

As the others gathered
to watch a small peak form on her body
not one among them

moved to claim
the crest of snow on the fallen girl's chest
as it rose. Sank and rose

She Speaks Only of Birds

Like the warbler, pierced by an arrow in Botswana
who followed the beacon now lodged in its breast
to the banks of the Oder— a small omen

of feather, stinkwood and iron—
She gasps at the jackdaws circling a corpse at day's end
One slip of the tongue and the whole murder will loathe us

She speaks of lories, who bicker in tropes
and the crowned eagles who sharpened their claws
on the spines of the Jews

Tonight I find her alone in the street, whistling like a bird
Don't rely on the thrushes, their song always changes
and never trust the starlings, ever shifting their shape

Since the Beginning of Time

Winter sits alone in the cold house
wearing a coat in need of dry cleaning
while she picks at a bowl of stiff oats
contemplating the warm bath she won't take
as she awaits his arrival. When Spring finally appears—
late again and preceded by a swarm
of love-drunk butterflies—he embraces
and hands her a fistful of lilies
Dear God not again! The same sweet blooms
he will toss the next day on her grave

Residue

Each generation learns from the previous,
so said my mother who never left the house

She would close herself up
in her bedroom for days, only to emerge

in a wig and a dress made of paper, on which
she had sketched vague faces

and landscapes with fat pieces of charcoal and spit
Once I thought I saw her in the street, a fur hat

and hooped earrings, eyes vacant
and no response to my call. *Doppelgänger*

she would say later, like the thick-boned villager
who helped load the trains

with mothers and daughters
then turned to the camera to swear

it wasn't her

Nighttime

The old nemeses gather, the bones
in my ears so small I can barely hear them
as they talk pitch and whistle
And who's this, but the San Andreas fault
full of snarl and strain, God knows what it's capable of
There's Marlene Dietrich again, insisting her wigs
be sprinkled with gold dust, and Picasso
shirtless and cruel in front of a masterpiece
I wish to settle it for once and for all—is it wrong to love
the art of the imperfect artist? Is the Tule truly
the thickest-trunked tree in the world? Surely
there are trunks yet unmeasured. The daikon
should taste as good as it sounds, though I feel
that it doesn't. I don't understand time dilation
though I know it involves travel to other planets, and still
no one has noticed my absence. Always
the proverbial lost cow without a bell

Immortality

A man gathers villagers and lines them up as if
they were bodies awaiting their turn to be buried
Nailed to the wall hangs
a faded cloth peony. There is a bench
for the apple-eyed children, chairs
for the haggard parents, the crones
and stooped men. Under a shroud
he focuses the lens. *Keep still, wretches!*
A small explosion, or perhaps
a spark of divine light
like the moment when seed joins egg
or a bite on this bitter winter day
of last summer's tomato

The House Built on Stilts

This house built on stilts is trying to keep its head above water
and so are we in these borrowed rooms where we watch

for waves, for cars and coyotes and that there are enough
cans of ravioli while remembering San Gennaro, the familiar

smell of sandal on asphalt and even the man we saw on the street
with a knife in his gut. They have taken a girl from her family

and put her in a box underground and we are forced to stay up
until 2:00 in the morning, the hour when even kidnappers

must sleep. We live in a scrum of dragged blankets and pillows
on the floor. We try the old trick with flashlights and mirrors, but

the tide has a mind of its own and we can't fool the moon
into setting nor convince the sea of the virtue of mercy

A Careless Cosmic Mistake

Our Days Were Numbered

Long before we considered our deaths, we lived
in a wagon filled with loose change
and old books. My mother wore long skirts
and danced for coins in the streets
while my father sold advice from the back of a wagon
Tired of life on the move, we settled
on a patch of dry land, slept in real beds
and ate meals off pages torn
from the calendar. June and July—
long bitter months of liver and spinach

The Raccoons

I can tell you nothing good was going on
but with raccoons nothing good ever is
They paced at night outside our house
in their stacked heels and leather
tossed bottles and butts in the grass
The worst wasn't the clatter of drums
or the mess they made when they went
through the trash, but the cruelty
with which they scattered
our bones in the street

What It Was Like

We were hunted like prey and forced to sleep under
the stars with venomous snakes. My father was adept
with a spear, although game back then was all gristle
and there was a key that hung from a string in the sky
but no doors

What We Learned About the Baby

Despite what we'd heard, she was not
made from mud. Nor was she a divine monster

or the homunculus, fully formed in the seed
She was not a root yanked from dirt, though when pulled

from a body she screamed like a mandrake
She was not a metaphor for the creator, not thought

perfected or purled in a spell, not holy equation—
her sum was less than we'd imagined. Her screams

were ancient songs that unsettled the birds,
made them clatter and thrash, then startled

the sculptor next door as he draped a thin veil
of skin over a small cage of rib

The Cats

They appeared at our door and we gave them names
like Isis, Saint Vicious and Froggy. They were fanatics
who'd lurk in the furnace ducts and tunnel through dirt
in the attic. Tangled in dolls' hair and bed sheets, they'd
howl and roam the halls in my mother's white night
gowns. Some were strung out, a few carried knives, one
kept a gun in a burlap sack. All were more menacing
than the worst radio gremlin

Under the Big Top

I didn't find growing up
in the circus to be easy
the daily splits and squats
the meals of old suet
long days being tossed in the air
then dropped on the ground
like the prey of bone-crushing birds

My father ran horses
with his bandy legs and a whip
while my mother did dishes
alone in the wagon
Those were strange times
because of the war
Tired of all the babies
lost along the way
she named me
Don't You Dare

For the Sake of My Name

Those days were different, names had just been invented
and the good ones were costly. The older generation

still remembered a time when people couldn't call their
unnamed children home for supper, and they endeavored

to buy the best. After Maria Rubio burned the face of Jesus
into a tortilla, my mother paid for my name working

long nights bent over a stove, feeding anonymous
starving children

For the New Parent

You will need hot water and towels
though what to do next is exactly unclear

Feed her noodles for dinner, cherries for dessert
Leave her there, on top of that tree, make sure

she doesn't fall off, the breaking of boughs
is strictly forbidden. Harsh words and discord

are not suitable for children and are to be avoided
Don't let her watch hours of grainy reruns

or carve her name in the front door. Make sure
the windows are screened, although screens

will be useless in the flood. Lock your closet and watch
for thieves, they have been known to steal

a young child and wear her mother's shoes
to cover their tracks

The Frogs

I despised their subtle villainy and love of citrus
the pretension of their brimmed hats and fringed vests
how they adored drive-in movies, packing their unbelted pups
in the back of the station wagon to watch devils and vampires
with the windows rolled up. Chain-smoking Marlboros
and drinking jugs of orange soda, slouched late at night in bars
on the beach, all slink and loose-limbed gyrations
as they danced in the shadows unashamed

A Thin Membrane

Though she never spoke of it, I knew she had a glass eye
but to confirm I asked her to touch her right eye
without flinching. To prove that my inquiry
was innocent, I raised my finger and pressed it
into my own eye, only to learn
that the landscape outside my skull
is a wilted field pocked with small clucking birds
in search of tiny kernels of corn,
none of them the least bit concerned
with the sky or its falling

The Return

After years of longing I went back to the yurt
in the village near Lake Baikal where we once lived
I spent cold and restless nights out on the steppe

well beyond the fine brick houses of Pravda Street
crouched over a fire drinking chai with mare's milk
Potatoes for dinner. Potatoes for lunch. Strum

an old tune on the balalaika, beat rugs with a stick.
The goats make a racket while the wind
blows the dirt back in your eyes

Home in Spanish

The house has a broken front door and a widowed earring—
the usual signs of ensuing loss. In the bathroom, a rusty tub

crazed tile floor, the bright coils of a family of scorpions
On the street a boy with a pigeon on his shoulder

My brother asks, *Do all the boys here get their own bird?*
The market is filled with knives and pyramids of chilis

At school I learn to say *home* in Spanish, nothing more
Outside, miles of saguaro and jumping cholla, a ribbon

of muddy water seeded with bodies. I count
three dead dogs, one dead horse and two children

singing as they pick through the garbage

And Finally, My Memoir

I ascribe no value to memory
The blue and yellow macaw is mostly grey
in the rendering, a once flushed neck
now anemic, no hint of musk in the recalling

The sound of a clock is not fully reheard,
not chime nor shuffle of the tiny man as he pops
out of his log house to remind us
that more time has been lost

My mother recalls that my birth was easy
due to an injection that made her forget pain
as well as the old family recipe
for making a golem

As a girl I was known to walk
with my head strolling two steps in front of me
like a careless cosmic mistake. Of course
I always forget what comes next

Concorde

My memory saturated after having remembered so much
I won't recall tomorrow what happens today
or how it once was you could leave London
at night and arrive in New York an hour before taking off
What happened to those precious minutes? It's not possible
that the sun can rise twice in one day, or that words
like knife and nipple and Tonton Macoute can tell the story
of a life. I try to answer the nagging question of why—
the best I can come up with is that I am here because this is where
everyone ends up, and like the others I will sit on the porch
and wait for the man on a unicycle who will lead
my funeral procession. But not yet: I am still on hold, trying
to reclaim my lost hour

On This Lost Planet

The Best Case Scenario

I wonder if the light I saw float
in the darkness the night you died

was the most sacred part of you
that had slipped through a pore

made its way to my house, into
my bedroom, past the drowsing cat

to wish me many good years
before you moved on to

wherever you were going—
and not an attempt

to settle the score, or worse
take me with you

Chiclets

I'd like not to die by fire or Great Devouring
and not like the man whose tongue

was removed by bandits, so he couldn't tell of
his unremarkable life. Instead let it be

at home and surrounded with googobs
of children, the youngest of whom

will clasp a doll and grow to be brave
like Juliane who fell 10,000 feet

still strapped to her seat, and survived
by chewing stale Chiclets for eleven days

in the jungle. Found, then free again
to ride her old click-clackety bike

The one with the broken chain

A Donkey's Dinner

Every book tries to explain how to cheat death
even the ones about dowsing, or those
dictated by God in a field
and etched on a cabbage. As a child
our school had only one book
which was placed on the floor
for us to read cross-legged in a circle,
half of us condemned for life
to read our books upside down

You can scare death away
with a scream, I read that in a book
though the fine print says
there are times death can't be frightened
in which case you must change your name to
Hugh or Apollo and forward your mail
to a fictitious address. In the last book I read
a woman joins a search party, staggers
into the dark woods with the others, only to realize
it is her name they are calling

The Unspeakable Illness Speaks

Don't cry, the body can't be preserved with tears
Think of it as a fire sale. Everyone Must Go!

Speaking of money— quarter, nickel, dime:
all as dead as a dollar now, pay them no

never-mind. That old dog? You can't take him
with you. No more questions! The music will

play you out. The hound starts to dig. The brass
raise their horns. I cross

to the other side of the street

A Crisis of Faith

I can't remember what I was named in my former life
and Ryan can't either, though he is certain
the street he once lived on decades ago
contains the word *Rock*. In his present incarnation he lives
in a small tidy house in Oklahoma

Ryan remembers dancing on stage for large crowds
the rush of applause, the chafe of his shoes
after a long run of shows, even the blowy deck
of the Queen Mary. Then there is the house—grand
with a pool, that he recalls with a longing that regularly

brings him to tears. His parents indulge him
with books about the theater that he scans for months
until he finds a photo of a man that he knows
to be his former self; a performer who lived in Beverly Hills
in a large house with a pool on Roxbury Drive

Ryan is not like the boy who lives now in Louisiana,
remembers dying after a gunfight and has a round birthmark
between his eyes to remind him of the bullet. Nor is he phobic
about water, like the girl now living in Atlanta, who recalls
drowning after a shipwreck on Lake Erie. Ryan's memories

fill him with pride. His only complaint is that in his present life
he has trouble learning to swim. I, on the other hand,
am perplexed by a God who would have a soul live
a good life, then make him start over pool-less in Tulsa

Like the Stars

Let me die like the stars
Make me explode, make me burn
and collapse

so my ash can seed
a fresh world
let my dust become the new core

Lord let them dig, let them dig

and then with my rust
let them paint the barns red

Since You Left

I imagine you walking in a white field
not in the clouds, but in tundra
and pulling a toboggan. You wear

sturdy boots, a fur hat like they wore in *Dr. Zhivago*,
where we learned that life is unkind
to soldiers and poets, worn out by history's

tumult and forced to search for their lost children
In the end, the lucky escape saber and gulag
and return home to master the balalaika

I have called you for years with no answer.
I can't help but think it has something to do with
that ridiculous hat

You Have Been Marked Absent Again

So many times I've tried to lure you back
with a bowl of warm milk and a whistle
like I would a kitten
or a child who lingers
too long in the bakery aisle

Longing is merely a sorrow that lurks
like the sullen truant smoking
outside the school gate, although
I understand your reluctance to leave the place
where I am told that every angel
is promised a pony

Benediction

I am not alone in thinking it can't be
that life is all thrill despite the excursions
and shapewear, the stars that throw color
across the sky like a disco ball. Aurora
or not, the huntress sitting on her horse,
falcon on her wrist, must contend with spoiled
milk and the specter of death. Never mind—
I will petition the heavens on all of our behalf
that when this is over we merit continued joy
a glass of hot tea, a spoonful of muskmelon jam
and all of our departed beloveds, together
on a plush carpet in God's finest tent

The Lilacs

It was not the moon we saw
but it outshone the lilacs
I had gone to gather with my father
I quickly forgot those voluptuous bushes
though they winked and bustled
as it hovered above the willows
Flying Saucer, he called it
as if it had slid out from under
a silo-sized teacup and flown off
the sun's breakfast table

Here, on this lost planet
my head remains turned to the sky

Acknowledgments

Enormous gratitude to Dick Lourie, an unfailingly kind and wise editor. Thank you to the teachers and early readers who helped shape these poems: Shane McCrae, Timothy Donnelly, Paul Muldoon, Lynn Melnick, David Kutz-Marks, Judith Hall, the late Richard Howard and the late Charles Simic. Thank you to my children, Isaac, Raina, Khaya and Josiah, and to my husband, Peter for love and encouragement.

Special thanks to Sherman Alexie for his wisdom and help.

Special thanks to the Haines family for the use of the painting, *Boy with Pigeons*, by Richard Haines, for the front cover.

Thank you also to the following journals where these poems have been published:

Broadkill Review: "What it Was Like"

Grist Journal: "The Big Top," "This is Off the Record"

Guesthouse: "She Speaks Only of Birds,"
  "What We Learned About the Baby"

Image Journal: "The Real McCoy"

Iterant: "Juana Maria," "A Donkey's Supper" and "The World's
  Loudest Sound"

New Ohio Review: "Residue"

Nimrod International Journal: "Always A Mercy," "The Concorde,"
  "And Finally, My Memoir"

Plume Poetry: "A Thin Membrane," "For The New Parent"

Western Humanities Review: "Adrift," "Dinner with the Oligarch"